Realistic Affirmations

FOR

WOMEN: SARCASTIC, HONEST

AND

DISAPPOINTING

by

Sandra Pollock

Realistic Affirmations for Women

© *2024 Sandra Pollock. All rights reserved.*

No part of this book may be reproduced, stored in a retrieval system, or transmitted in any form or by any means—electronic, mechanical, photocopying, recording, or otherwise—without prior written permission from the author, except for brief quotations in a book review or other critical work.

This book is a work of nonfiction. It is intended to inspire and empower readers, but it is not a substitute for professional advice. The author and publisher disclaim any liability arising from the use or misuse of the information in this book.

1

"I am letting go of the past... unless it's a grudge, because some things are worth holding onto."

They say letting go is freeing, but honestly, holding onto a well-earned grudge can be pretty motivating. A little pettiness, when channeled correctly, is the ultimate productivity hack. That person who doubted me in high school? Fuel. The co-worker who stole credit for my idea? Pure inspiration. I'm not bitter—I'm driven. Today, I'll remind myself that grudges aren't necessarily unhealthy; they're just deeply personal motivational strategies. After all, there's nothing wrong with succeeding while imagining the look on someone's face when they realize they underestimated you.

Action Plan: Think of one grudge that inspires you. Use it to fuel a productive action today and celebrate your victorious pettiness.

2

"I am worthy of success, even if I Google how to do my job every day."

Imposter syndrome? Never heard of her. Well, maybe I have... every day. But here's the truth: no one really knows what they're doing 100% of the time. We're all just stringing together information from Google, YouTube tutorials, and random Reddit threads to make it through. The real skill is in making it look effortless while hiding your search history. Success isn't about having all the answers—it's about knowing where to find them and convincing everyone else you had them all along.

Action Plan: Pick one daunting task that's been hanging over you. Instead of panicking, type it into Google like a pro and find a step-by-step solution.

Remind yourself that even experts started with "How to..." searches. Bonus points if you share your newfound knowledge and pretend you've known it forever.

3

"I am embracing balance... by scrolling Instagram while pretending to work."

Work-life balance is a noble goal, but sometimes balance looks more like holding your phone under the desk while nodding in agreement during a Zoom call. Sure, I could power through my to-do list uninterrupted, but where's the fun in that? Social media breaks are practically medicinal—they give me a quick dopamine hit and the illusion that I'm connecting with the world, even if it's just memes. Balance doesn't mean perfection; it means sneaking in tiny moments of joy wherever you can find them.

Action Plan: Give yourself permission for a guiltfree scroll session today. Set a timer for five minutes, dive into your favorite app, and enjoy the mental break. Afterward, tackle your next task with renewed focus... or at least a fun new meme to share at lunch.

4

"I am perfectly capable of handling today's nonsense... one coffee at a time."

Let's not kid ourselves—I'm not tackling today's challenges out of sheer motivation or boundless energy. No, today's nonsense will be met head-on with caffeine and stubborn resolve. Coffee doesn't just fuel my body; it powers my soul, transforms grumbles into semi-coherent words, and helps me tolerate questionable decisions made by others. Every sip is a reminder that I'm one step closer to surviving the chaos. Sure, they say water is essential for life, but let's be honest: water doesn't come in a caramel latte.

Action Plan: Brew your favorite cup of coffee or tea—or grab one on the way to your next meeting. Take a deep breath, savor the first sip, and mentally prepare to deal with today's inevitable absurdities. If things still go sideways, remind yourself there's always a second cup (or third).

5

"I am confident in my decisions... even when they involve carbs for dinner again."

Carbs aren't just food; they're a love language, a warm hug, and a survival strategy. Sure, I could try a low-carb lifestyle, but why would I deprive myself of one of life's simplest pleasures? Pasta doesn't judge me for my life choices, and bread never expects me to have it all figured out. Today, I remind myself that self-care doesn't always look like kale smoothies and yoga classes. Sometimes, it's buttery garlic bread and unapologetically clearing my plate. Balance is overrated; happiness, however, is not.

Action Plan: Plan a meal today that brings you pure joy, whether it's comfort food, a sweet treat, or both. Savor every bite without guilt, and remind yourself that nourishment is about more than just fuel—it's about enjoying life, one delicious carb at a time.

6

"I am embracing the chaos because pretending it's under control is exhausting."

Life is messy, and that's okay. Today, I'll stop wasting energy trying to make everything look perfect and just go with the flow. Chaos isn't the enemy—it's proof that I'm doing my best to juggle life's demands. Besides, perfection is boring, and chaos keeps things interesting.

Action Plan: Accept one thing today that's out of your control. Laugh at the absurdity of it and remind yourself that sometimes "good enough" is exactly right.

7

"I am confident in my ability to make mistakes—and learn from at least half of them."

Mistakes are inevitable, but they're also where the best lessons come from. Today, I'll remind myself that perfection is overrated, and learning is what really matters. If I can laugh at my missteps along the way, even better. Growth doesn't happen without a little trial and error.

Action Plan: Reflect on one recent mistake. Write down what you learned from it and how you can apply that lesson moving forward. Bonus: forgive yourself for the other half you didn't learn from.

8

"I am giving myself credit for showing up, even if that's the only thing I accomplish today."

Some days, just getting out of bed is a victory. Today, I'll remind myself that showing up—whether for work, family, or just myself—is an act of courage. Even if I accomplish nothing else, I've already done enough. Showing up is the first step toward anything meaningful.

Action Plan: Acknowledge one area where you showed up today, even if it was just getting through a tough moment. Take a minute to celebrate that effort—it counts.

9

"I am fully capable of adulting, even if I secretly Google 'how to adult' sometimes."

Adulting isn't always intuitive, and no one gave me a manual. Today, I'll remind myself that figuring things out as I go is part of the process. Everyone is improvising their way through life, and I'm doing just fine—even if I do need to Google how to fold a fitted sheet.

Action Plan: Tackle one "adulting" task you've been avoiding, like paying a bill or fixing something. When it's done, give yourself credit for being an unofficial expert in figuring life out.

10

"I am a multitasking genius... or at least convincing enough that no one notices otherwise."

Multitasking is an art, and I've mastered the appearance of doing it all—whether or not that's true. Today, I'll remind myself that managing priorities is about survival, not perfection. Sometimes, the secret to multitasking is just looking busy and hoping for the best.

Action Plan: Choose one priority to fully focus on for an hour today. Forget juggling—dedicate your energy to one task and enjoy the rare feeling of productivity.

11

"I am embracing progress, even if it's just baby steps in the right direction."

Not every day will be a giant leap forward, and that's okay. Today, I'll remind myself that even small progress is still progress. Each step, no matter how tiny, gets me closer to where I want to be. Slow and steady wins... well, maybe not the race, but definitely some personal peace.

Action Plan: Identify one small step you can take today toward a goal, no matter how insignificant it seems. Celebrate that step like it's a marathon finish line.

12

"I am fully prepared to fake confidence until I start believing it myself."

Confidence isn't something I'm born with—it's something I practice. Today, I'll remind myself that pretending I've got it together is half the battle. If I keep showing up and acting like I belong, sooner or later, I'll actually believe it. Bonus: everyone else is probably faking it too.

Action Plan: Walk into one situation today with your best "I've got this" face, even if you're not sure you do. Channel that energy until it feels real.

13

"I am embracing my quirks because normal is overrated."

I wasn't born to blend in, and that's a good thing. Today, I'll remind myself that my quirks make me interesting, unique, and memorable. Who wants to be normal, anyway? Life is too short to worry about fitting into a box that was never meant for me.

Action Plan: Write down one thing that makes you "weird" or unique. Celebrate it as a part of what makes you, you. Bonus points if you share it with someone who appreciates it.

14

"I am capable of getting things done, even if I'm doing them at the last minute."

Procrastination doesn't mean I'm lazy—it means I work well under pressure. Today, I'll remind myself that last-minute miracles are still miracles. My ability to pull it all together at the eleventh hour is nothing short of impressive, even if I secretly promise myself to start earlier next time.

Action Plan: Take one task you've been avoiding and break it into small chunks. Knock out just one chunk today and pat yourself on the back for "early" progress.

15

"I am not responsible for everyone's happiness, just my own sanity."

I can't please everyone, and that's not my job anyway. Today, I'll remind myself that my mental health matters more than anyone else's unrealistic expectations. Taking care of myself isn't selfish—it's necessary. The happier I am, the better I can show up for the people I care about.

Action Plan: Set a boundary in one area of your life today, whether it's saying no or prioritizing alone time. Remind yourself it's okay to put your sanity first.

16

"I am not 'too much'—the world just needs to catch up."

My passion, energy, and drive are assets, not flaws. Today, I'll remind myself that I don't have to shrink myself to make others comfortable. If someone thinks I'm too much, that's their problem, not mine. I'll keep showing up fully and unapologetically as myself.

Action Plan: Write down one thing you've been told is "too much" about you. Reflect on how it's actually one of your strengths, and embrace it today with pride.

17

"I am perfectly capable of resting without feeling guilty... probably."

Resting doesn't make me lazy; it makes me human. Today, I'll remind myself that taking a break isn't a weakness—it's a reset. Sure, I might feel a twinge of guilt, but I'll do it anyway because rest is the fuel that keeps me going.

Action Plan: Schedule a guilt-free rest break today. Use the time to recharge, even if it's just 15 minutes of doing absolutely nothing.

18

"I am strong enough to handle whatever nonsense today throws my way."

Every day has its challenges, and today will be no exception. But I'll remind myself that I've survived every ridiculous curveball life has thrown at me so far. If I can handle yesterday's chaos, I can handle today's too—with grace, grit, and maybe some snacks.

Action Plan: Think of one tough situation you've conquered recently. Use it as proof that you can take on anything today.

19

"I am the queen of multitasking, even if most of it is mental gymnastics."

Sure, I'm juggling 10 things at once, but I've mastered the art of pretending it's all under control. Today, I'll remind myself that multitasking isn't about perfection—it's about survival. Whether I'm actually productive or just appearing busy, I'm doing the best I can.

Action Plan: Focus on completing just one task today, even if it's tiny. Let yourself off the hook for juggling everything else at the same time.

20

"I am absolutely thriving... if thriving means wearing pants and showing up."

Let's not overcomplicate things. Today, I'll remind myself that showing up—physically or mentally—is already an achievement. Thriving doesn't have to mean perfect hair or a spotless to-do list.

Sometimes, thriving is simply surviving, one pair of pants at a time.

Action Plan: Celebrate one small victory today, even if it's just making it through the day. Write it down as proof that you're thriving in your own way.

21

"I am fully aware that 'winging it' is my preferred strategy."

Let's face it: detailed planning isn't always my forte. Today, I'll embrace the art of improvisation. Who needs a roadmap when spontaneity keeps life interesting? After all, some of the best moments happen when I just go with the flow and trust myself to figure things out as I go along.

Action Plan: Tackle one task today without overthinking it. Dive in and trust your instincts—you might be pleasantly surprised by the outcome.

"I am accepting that my to-do list is more of a suggestion than a mandate."

My to-do list is ambitious, but let's be honest—it's more of a wishlist. Today, I'll remind myself that it's okay if not everything gets checked off. Life happens, priorities shift, and sometimes the couch just looks too inviting. Productivity is flexible, and so am I.

Action Plan: Choose the top three most important tasks on your list and focus on those. Let the rest roll over to another day without guilt.

23

"I am embracing the fact that 'good enough' is sometimes truly good enough."

Perfection is exhausting and often unnecessary. Today, I'll accept that doing a decent job is perfectly acceptable. Not every task needs to be a masterpiece; sometimes, getting it done is what matters most. I'll save my energy for the things that truly require extra effort.

Action Plan: Complete a task today without obsessing over every detail. Submit it proudly, knowing that your best effort for today is enough.

24

"I am choosing to ignore the laundry—it will still be there tomorrow."

Laundry is like a clingy ex—it just won't go away. Today, I'll prioritize something more enjoyable, knowing that the laundry can wait. Life is too short to be ruled by chores that never end. I'll take this time to do something that actually brings me joy.

Action Plan: Instead of tackling laundry today, spend that time on a hobby or relaxing activity. Remind yourself that self-care is just as important as housework.

25

"I am fully prepared to handle any crisis— after my morning coffee."

Emergencies can wait until I'm adequately caffeinated. Today, I'll acknowledge that I'm not at my best until I've had that first cup. It's not procrastination; it's ensuring I'm in the right mindset to tackle whatever comes my way. Priorities, right?

Action Plan: Take a moment to enjoy your morning beverage without rushing. Use this time to mentally prepare for the day ahead.

26

"I am accepting that sometimes the best plan is no plan at all."

Overplanning can lead to disappointment when things inevitably go off course. Today, I'll embrace spontaneity and see where the day takes me. Flexibility can lead to unexpected opportunities and a lot less stress. Besides, plans are just ideas that can be changed.

Action Plan: Leave one part of your day unscheduled. Allow yourself to do whatever feels right in the moment and enjoy the freedom it brings.

27

"I am acknowledging that 'later' is a perfectly acceptable time to get things done."

Procrastination gets a bad rap, but sometimes delaying tasks is just prioritizing in disguise. Today, I'll accept that not everything needs immediate attention. I'll focus on what feels most important now and leave the rest for later—without any guilt.

Action Plan: Identify a non-urgent task that's been nagging at you. Give yourself permission to postpone it and focus on what truly needs your attention today.

28

"I am embracing my inner child—tantrums and all."

Sometimes adulting is overrated. Today, I'll allow myself to express my frustrations, even if it's with a bit of flair. Letting out emotions can be healthy, and who says I can't indulge in a little stomp or sigh? It's all part of processing and moving on.

Action Plan: If you feel overwhelmed today, take a moment to vent—write it down, say it out loud, or have a mini dance-off. Then, proceed with your day feeling lighter.

29

"I am recognizing that talking to myself is just a staff meeting with my best advisor."

Self-talk isn't weird; it's effective communication with someone who truly understands me—me!

Today, I'll engage in thoughtful conversations with myself to sort out my thoughts. It's brainstorming at its finest, and I'm the CEO of my own mind.

Action Plan: Spend a few minutes today "talking" through a problem or idea with yourself. Use this time to clarify your thoughts without judgment.

30

"I am accepting that adulting is like folding a fitted sheet—no one really knows how."

Life doesn't come with instructions, and most of us are just making it up as we go along. Today, I'll cut myself some slack for not having all the answers. It's okay to stumble through and learn along the way. Imperfection is the human condition, after all.

Action Plan: When faced with uncertainty today, remind yourself that it's normal not to know everything. Embrace the learning process and take it one step at a time.

31

"I am choosing not to stress about things I've already forgotten to do."

If I can't remember it, it probably wasn't that important. Today, I'll remind myself that worrying about forgotten tasks won't bring them back. Instead, I'll focus on what's in front of me and let the past slip quietly into the abyss of my mind's "deleted files."

Action Plan: Write down the top three tasks you need to focus on today. Let the rest go, knowing that you're doing what truly matters right now.

32

"I am a work in progress—and so is my email inbox."

Both me and my inbox are messy, and that's okay. Today, I'll remind myself that perfection isn't the goal—progress is. Whether it's clearing one email or making one small change, I'm doing enough. Rome wasn't built in a day, and neither is inbox zero.

Action Plan: Sort or delete five emails today. Celebrate the small win and remind yourself there's always tomorrow for the rest.

33

"I am totally fine with starting the day over at 3 p.m."

Some days don't go as planned, and that's perfectly fine. Today, I'll remind myself that it's never too late to reset. The morning may have been a disaster, but I've still got the afternoon to turn things around—or at least get through it with fewer eye rolls.

Action Plan: Take a five-minute break, stretch, and set a small goal for the rest of your day. Treat 3 p.m. like a fresh start.

34

"I am accepting that laundry is less of a chore and more of a lifelong commitment."

No matter how many loads I do, it always comes back. Today, I'll stop fighting the endless cycle of laundry and accept it as part of life. Instead of stressing about it, I'll find small ways to make it tolerable—like listening to a podcast while folding socks.

Action Plan: Pick one small step for tackling laundry today—start a load, fold a few items, or simply shove it out of sight for now. Progress, not perfection.

35

"I am brave enough to take on today... after a few motivational pep talks with myself."

Before I conquer the world, I'll have a word with my most trusted advisor: me. Today, I'll remind myself that there's no shame in needing a little encouragement. Sometimes, hyping myself up in the mirror is all I need to take on whatever life throws my way.

Action Plan: Start your day with a mini pep talk. Look in the mirror and remind yourself of one thing you're awesome at, no matter how small.

36

"I am allowing myself to be a little extra, because why not?"

Life is too short to dim my sparkle for anyone else. Today, I'll remind myself that being "extra" isn't a flaw—it's a feature. Whether it's wearing bold colors, taking a long lunch, or treating myself to dessert, I'll embrace my extra-ness with pride.

Action Plan: Do one thing today that feels a little indulgent or bold, whether it's ordering your favorite latte or wearing that statement accessory. Own it.

37

"I am proud of myself for not hitting 'reply all' by mistake."

Sometimes success is just avoiding disaster, and today I'll celebrate the little victories. Whether it's sending an email to the right person or remembering to mute myself on Zoom, I'll remind myself that these tiny wins are just as important as the big ones.

Action Plan: Reflect on one small, almost unnoticeable thing you did right today. Pat yourself on the back for saving yourself a headache.

38

"I am fully prepared to survive today's drama with snacks and sarcasm."

Drama may be inevitable, but so is my ability to deal with it. Today, I'll remind myself that snacks, a sharp sense of humor, and a deep well of sarcasm are my secret weapons. If all else fails, I'll chew loudly to drown out the nonsense.

Action Plan: Pack your favorite snack and arm yourself with a sarcastic one-liner for the day's challenges. Survival looks delicious.

39

"I am perfectly capable of doing nothing productive today—and calling it self-care."

Sometimes rest is revolutionary, or at least that's what I'll tell myself. Today, I'll embrace the art of doing absolutely nothing while pretending it's for my mental health.

Action Plan: Cancel one thing on your to-do list and replace it with a guilt-free nap or Netflix binge. You've earned it.

40

"I am embracing the power of small wins— like remembering to water the plants."

Big achievements are great, but so are the tiny ones. Today, I'll remind myself that progress is made up of little victories. If I water my plants, answer one email, or remember to take my vitamins, I'll celebrate those wins like I just climbed Mount Everest.

Action Plan: Write down three small wins at the end of the day, no matter how minor. Reflect on how those small moments add up to progress.

41

"I am thriving... if thriving means remembering to feed myself today."

Bare minimum counts as success, right? Today, I'll remind myself that a sandwich is basically gourmet, and surviving is an accomplishment in itself.

Action Plan: Make yourself a simple meal, call it a masterpiece, and celebrate the fact that you didn't forget to eat today.

42

"I am not overthinking—I'm just exploring every possible way this could go wrong."

My brain is basically a 24/7 worst-case scenario generator. Today, I'll accept that my overthinking is just creativity with anxiety as a sidekick.

Action Plan: Write down your most ridiculous "what if" scenario, then laugh at how absurd

43

"I am perfectly capable of achieving greatness... as long as greatness involves staying in bed until noon."

The world can wait—I'm prioritizing rest today. After all, legends don't rush their rise to fame.

Action Plan: Cancel your morning plans (or just pretend you had some), stay cozy, and enjoy the luxury of doing nothing before noon.

44

"I am not lazy—I'm just highly efficient at conserving energy."

Why waste energy doing something now when it could be done tomorrow? Today, I'll remind myself that procrastination is really just strategic rest.

Action Plan: Pick one task and delay it until tomorrow with zero guilt. Use the free time to perfect your energy-saving skills.

45

"I am fully committed to being semicommitted to my goals."

Dreams take time, and I'm taking the scenic route. Today, I'll remind myself that slow progress is still progress—especially when paired with long breaks.

Action Plan: Pick one goal to work on today, even if it's just brainstorming. Celebrate any effort, no matter how minimal.

46

"I am capable of handling whatever comes my way—so long as it doesn't involve group projects."

Collaboration is overrated when I can clearly do it all myself. Today, I'll remind myself that teamwork is just another way of testing my patience.

Action Plan: Politely decline one group activity today. Enjoy the peace of working solo while pretending it's a productivity hack.

47

"I am okay with being a hot mess because at least I'm a lovable one."

Perfection is boring, but I'm not. Today, I'll remind myself that life's quirks make me interesting—even if those quirks include losing my keys five times a day.

Action Plan: Laugh at one thing you "messed up" today. Share the story with a friend—it might make their day, too.

48

"I am perfectly fine with lowering the bar when necessary—like today."

Expectations are stressful, so I'm choosing to set mine at ankle height. Today, I'll remind myself that surviving the day is more than enough.

Action Plan: Pick one task to downgrade from "perfect" to "good enough." Let the pressure go and enjoy the relief.

49

"I am smart enough to Google the answers and pretend I knew them all along."

Knowledge isn't about knowing everything—it's about knowing how to find it on the internet. Today, I'll remind myself that Google is my real brain.

Action Plan: Look up something you've been avoiding because it seemed complicated. Bask in the glory of pretending you knew it all along.

50

"I am choosing to give myself grace... because nobody else seems to be offering it."

The world can be tough, but I can be kind to myself. Today, I'll remind myself that I don't have to be perfect to be lovable—or to deserve dessert.

Action Plan: Treat yourself to something indulgent today, whether it's a snack, a nap, or ignoring your inbox for an hour.

51

"I am fully embracing the power of pretending I know what I'm doing."

Confidence is 90% attitude and 10% Googling the answers. Today, I'll remind myself that no one has it all figured out, and that's okay. Pretending I have a clue is a skill in itself, and I'll lean into it until I eventually do know what I'm doing.

Action Plan: Approach one challenge today with confidence, even if you're unsure of the outcome. Trust that you'll figure it out as you go.

52

"I am reminding myself that self-care doesn't have to involve kale."

Not all self-care looks like green smoothies and yoga. Today, I'll remind myself that self-care is anything that makes me feel good—whether it's a long nap, binge-watching a show, or eating my weight in chocolate. Whatever works for me is the right kind of care.

Action Plan: Treat yourself to something today that brings you comfort, no matter how small or indulgent it may seem.

53

"I am ready to face the day... as soon as I figure out what day it actually is."

Time is an illusion, and calendars are overrated. Today, I'll remind myself that showing up is half the battle—even if I show up slightly confused.

Action Plan: Double-check the date and your schedule. Laugh at yourself for forgetting (again), then confidently tackle whatever comes next

54

"I am accepting that socks will never truly match, and that's fine."

Some battles aren't worth fighting, and socks are one of them. Today, I'll remind myself that life is too short to worry about the little things. If mismatched socks or imperfect plans are my biggest problems, I'm probably doing okay.

Action Plan: Find humor in one minor inconvenience today. Laugh it off and move on—you have bigger things to conquer.

55

"I am accepting that my social battery is at 2%, and that's okay."

People are great, but silence is better. Today, I'll remind myself that it's perfectly fine to dodge small talk and recharge alone.

Action Plan: Set aside some alone time today, even if it's just a 10-minute walk. Use the peace to mentally hit "reset."

56

"I am embracing the fact that my inbox will never truly be empty."

Inbox zero is a myth created to torment me. Today, I'll remind myself that unanswered emails are just proof that people think I'm important.

Action Plan: Answer one email you've been avoiding and leave the rest for tomorrow—or next week. Priorities, right?

57

"I am fine with not being everyone's cup of tea—I'm more of a coffee person anyway."

Not everyone will like me, and that's okay. Today, I'll remind myself that I'm not here to cater to everyone's tastes. I'm here to be unapologetically me.

Action Plan: Think of one thing that makes you unique and celebrate it unapologetically. Bonus points if you share it with someone.

58

"I am choosing to see my procrastination as a sign of creative genius."

Procrastinating isn't laziness—it's just my brain marinating ideas. Today, I'll remind myself that waiting until the last minute only makes me more efficient under pressure.

Action Plan: Pick one task you've been procrastinating and set a timer for 15 minutes. Start small and see where it leads.

59

"I am strong enough to deal with difficult people... after I've rolled my eyes at them."

Patience doesn't mean I don't get annoyed—it just means I hide it well. Today, I'll remind myself that eye rolls are harmless if no one sees them.

Action Plan: The next time someone tests your patience, take a deep breath and count to three before responding. Bonus: roll your eyes internally for instant relief.

60

"I am embracing my imperfections because they make me human."

Perfection is boring, and flaws are what make me real. Today, I'll remind myself that my imperfections don't define me—they make me unique, relatable, and whole. I'll celebrate the parts of me that are beautifully imperfect, just like everyone else.

Action Plan: Reflect on one "imperfection" you've been critical of. Reframe it as a strength or simply accept it as part of your authentic self.

61

"I am accepting that my to-do list is more of a 'maybe later' list."

My to-do list might be ambitious, but it's really more of a wishlist. Today, I'll remind myself that priorities change, and that's perfectly okay.

Action Plan: Choose the one most important task on your list and focus only on that. Let the rest roll over to another day without guilt.

62

"I am proud of myself for resisting the urge to throw my computer out the window."

Technology has its limits—and so do I. Today, I'll remind myself that smashing things isn't productive, even if it feels satisfying in the moment.

Action Plan: When faced with tech trouble today, step away for five minutes. Come back with fresh eyes (and maybe fewer destructive impulses).

63

"I am confidently ignoring advice I didn't ask for today."

Unsolicited advice is just background noise. Today, I'll remind myself that I don't have to explain or justify my choices to anyone who feels like offering their two cents.

Action Plan: Politely tune out the next piece of unsolicited advice you receive. Smile, nod, and mentally change the subject.

64

"I am fully embracing the fact that socks are optional."

Who needs socks anyway? Today, I'll remind myself that life is too short to stress about matching accessories—especially when I can go sock-free and save laundry time.

Action Plan: Skip one unnecessary task today, whether it's finding matching socks or replying to that annoying email. Enjoy the freedom.

65

"I am okay with the fact that my 'five-minute break' might turn into an hour."

Time is a suggestion, not a rule. Today, I'll remind myself that a little extra rest isn't procrastination—it's a strategic recharge.

Action Plan: Take a break today without setting a timer. See how long it feels good to rest before getting back to work.

66

"I am fully prepared to fake it until I eventually feel like I've got this."

Confidence is just acting like you know what you're doing until you actually do. Today, I'll remind myself that everyone is faking it to some degree—so I might as well join in.

Action Plan: Approach one task today with an air of confidence, even if you feel clueless. Pretend you've got it together, and it might just work.

67

"I am accepting that cleaning one corner of the room is basically the same as cleaning the whole house."

Why clean everything when I can just tidy up the parts people see? Today, I'll remind myself that strategic cleaning is the only cleaning that matters.

Action Plan: Pick one small area to clean or organize today. Leave the rest for "later" (or never).

68

"I am giving myself permission to laugh at my own awkwardness."

Awkward moments are just proof that I'm human. Today, I'll remind myself that laughing at myself is way better than cringing forever. Besides, awkward makes life interesting.

Action Plan: The next time you trip over your words (or your own feet), laugh it off and move on. Share the story with someone who'll find it funny too.

69

"I am not responsible for everyone else's happiness—it's a full-time job just managing my own."

Trying to please everyone is exhausting, and today, I'll remind myself that I'm not a one-person happiness factory. People can handle their own joy while I focus on mine.

Action Plan: Say no to one unnecessary request today. Use the extra time to do something that actually makes you happy.

70

"I am celebrating my ability to keep it together—even if it's just barely."

Some days, survival is the real victory. Today, I'll remind myself that holding it all together, even by a thread, is still an impressive feat.

Action Plan: Reflect on one small way you kept it together today, no matter how minor. Reward yourself with something comforting or indulgent.

71

"I am choosing to believe that chaos is just another form of creativity."

Messy desk? Creative genius. Cluttered schedule? Spontaneous brilliance. Today, I'll remind myself that chaos is just the art of living loudly.

Action Plan: Leave one mess untouched today and call it a "creative workspace." Use the time saved to enjoy something fun.

72

"I am okay with answering emails in my pajamas—it's called work-life balance."

Comfort doesn't take away from productivity; it enhances it. Today, I'll remind myself that my attire doesn't determine my worth—unless it's a cape, then I'm extra worthy.

Action Plan: Work from your coziest spot today, whether that's the couch, the bed, or the floor. Bonus points for wearing fuzzy socks.

73

"I am accepting that I'm a morning person only in theory."

Mornings sound great on paper, but reality disagrees. Today, I'll remind myself that I can still have a productive day even if it starts after 10 a.m.

Action Plan: Skip the early alarm tomorrow. Let yourself sleep in and start the day when your body says it's ready.

74

"I am proud of myself for not responding to stupidity with stupidity."

It's tempting, but today, I'll remind myself that staying calm in the face of nonsense is the ultimate power move. My silence speaks volumes—and it's much louder than their bad opinions.

Action Plan: The next time someone tests your patience, take a deep breath and let their nonsense pass. Congratulate yourself for taking the high road.

75

"I am perfectly fine with being a little dramatic—it's part of my charm."

Life's too short to play it cool all the time. Today, I'll remind myself that a little extra flair never hurt anyone. Besides, what's the point of a story if it's not entertaining?

Action Plan: Add a touch of drama to your day, whether it's a dramatic pause in a conversation or an Oscar-worthy sigh. Own it unapologetically.

76

"I am embracing the fact that the laundry will never be done—and that's okay."

It's not procrastination; it's a lifestyle choice.

Today, I'll remind myself that laundry is a battle I'm not interested in winning. Clean clothes are optional anyway.

Action Plan: Shove the laundry into a basket and move on with your life. Tomorrow's a new day (for the same pile).

"I am choosing not to let one bad moment ruin my entire day—probably."

A single mishap isn't the end of the world. Today, I'll remind myself that bad moments are just that:

moments. I'll keep moving forward, even if I grumble along the way.

Action Plan: When something goes wrong today, take a deep breath and say, "Well, that happened." Then get back to doing your thing.

78

"I am smart enough to know when to let someone else take the blame."

Not every mistake needs my name attached to it. Today, I'll remind myself that staying quiet while someone else volunteers for the guilt is a form of self-preservation.

Action Plan: The next time something minor goes wrong, let someone else swoop in with their unsolicited "fix." Step back and enjoy the show.

79

"I am proud of myself for keeping my sarcasm in check... most of the time."

Sarcasm is my second language, but today, I'll remind myself that not everyone appreciates it. I'll practice the art of self-control—at least until the next overly dramatic situation.

Action Plan: Save one sarcastic comment today by keeping it to yourself. Reward your restraint with chocolate or a snarky meme.

80

"I am fully embracing the fact that forgetting why I walked into a room is just part of my journey."

My brain might have the attention span of a goldfish, but at least it keeps things interesting. Today, I'll remind myself that I'm not forgetful—I'm spontaneous.

Action Plan: The next time you forget what you were doing, laugh it off and do something else entirely. Call it an unplanned adventure.

81

"I am accepting that my life is a mix of Pinterest dreams and Amazon Prime realities."

Sure, I have big aspirations, but practicality wins every time. Today, I'll remind myself that it's okay if my vision board doesn't match my shopping cart.

Action Plan: Celebrate one small, practical win today, whether it's cooking a simple meal or finally ordering that thing you've been putting off.

82

"I am proud of myself for not saying what I'm really thinking—again."

Self-restraint is a superpower, and today, I'll remind myself that keeping my thoughts to myself saves me from unnecessary drama. My inner monologue deserves an award.

Action Plan: Write down one sarcastic thought you had today but didn't say out loud. Smile knowing you dodged a potential mess.

83

"I am fully prepared to solve the day's problems—as long as they don't involve math."

Numbers? No, thank you. Today, I'll remind myself that not every challenge requires me to engage with my arch-nemesis: basic arithmetic.

Action Plan: When faced with a math-related issue, delegate it to someone else. Your gift to the world is creativity, not calculations.

84

"I am choosing to see deadlines as more of a friendly suggestion."

Deadlines exist to give me a sense of urgency—eventually. Today, I'll remind myself that great things take time, even if that time includes lastminute panic.

Action Plan: Work on one deadline today, but leave just enough to finish it "heroically" at the last minute. Bask in the rush.

85

"I am okay with letting my phone battery die—it's called living off the grid."

Sometimes, disconnecting is the ultimate act of self-care (or laziness). Today, I'll remind myself that the world can survive without me answering texts immediately.

Action Plan: Put your phone on silent for an hour. Ignore notifications and enjoy the peaceful illusion of being unreachable.

86

"I am accepting that my plants and I are both just trying our best to stay alive."

My plants may look thirsty, but so do I. Today, I'll remind myself that survival—whether for me or my greenery—is a shared victory.

Action Plan: Water your plants today. Bonus: Drink a glass of water yourself. Consider it teamwork.

87

"I am celebrating the fact that I managed to do laundry without shrinking anything."

Small victories are still victories, and today, I'll remind myself that completing a household chore without a disaster is basically winning at life.

Action Plan: Fold one load of laundry while blasting your favorite song. Call it a moment of pure adulting bliss.

88

"I am okay with the fact that my car doubles as a mobile trash can."

Who needs a spotless vehicle when it's basically an extension of my life? Today, I'll remind myself that cluttered cars have character—and snacks in the glove box are a bonus.

Action Plan: Remove one piece of trash from your car today. Congratulate yourself on making progress without going overboard.

89

"I am reminding myself that yoga pants are for everything—except yoga."

Comfort is a priority, and I'll embrace my stretchy, versatile wardrobe for all occasions. Today, I'll remind myself that yoga pants can handle errands, lounging, and existential crises, all without breaking a sweat.

Action Plan: Wear your comfiest outfit today, even if it's just for lounging. Celebrate the genius of fashion-meets-function.

90

"I am fully embracing the idea that 'clean enough' is an actual standard of cleanliness."

My home doesn't need to sparkle—it just needs to not look like a crime scene. Today, I'll remind myself that 'clean enough' means I've already done more than necessary.

Action Plan: Tidy one thing today and leave the rest. Celebrate the fact that your house isn't on a reality show about hoarders.

91

"I am perfectly fine with having a fridge full of condiments and no actual food."

Who needs full meals when I've got endless flavor options? Today, I'll remind myself that my ketchup collection is a form of culinary creativity.

Action Plan: Make a game out of using one of the random condiments in your fridge today. Call it gourmet experimentation.

92

"I am okay with celebrating small victories— like parallel parking on the first try."

Forget the big stuff; today, I'll remind myself that nailing the little things is just as satisfying. Who needs a promotion when I've conquered the curb?

Action Plan: Recognize one "tiny triumph" from today and treat yourself to a victory dance—or a snack.

93

"I am strong enough to not cry when my phone screen cracks—barely."

Material things don't define me, but my phone almost does. Today, I'll remind myself that a cracked screen doesn't mean my life is shattered—it just looks that way.

Action Plan: If disaster strikes, research a fix (or slap on a screen protector and pretend it's fine).Bonus: Take deep breaths first.

94

"I am reminding myself that gym memberships are basically just donations to the fitness industry."

Sure, I'll get there... eventually. Today, I'll remind myself that signing up was the hard part, and the thought of exercise totally counts as progress.

Action Plan: Take a short walk today and call it "getting back into fitness." Celebrate with a snack for balance.

95

"I am okay with the fact that every meeting could have been an email."

Why say in 30 minutes what you could write in five? Today, I'll remind myself that pointless meetings are just free thinking time for my next great idea—or grocery list.

Action Plan: During your next unnecessary meeting, jot down something fun or creative instead of stressing over the agenda.

96

"I am choosing to believe that my laundry pile is a work of modern art."

Who's to say it's not intentional? Today, I'll remind myself that my "Mount Washmore" is just an abstract representation of life's endless cycles.

Action Plan: Fold two things from the pile today. Leave the rest as your ongoing masterpiece.

"I am perfectly capable of taking a walk—right to my fridge and back."

Exercise is relative, and today I'll remind myself that a snack run counts as cardio. Every step matters, even if it's for chips.

Action Plan: Take a mini walk today, even if it's just to your kitchen. Pair it with something fun, like picking your favorite treat.

98

"I am totally fine with the fact that my online shopping cart is basically my dream journal."

Buying it is optional; dreaming about it is mandatory. Today, I'll remind myself that curating a perfect cart is its own reward—and much cheaper.

Action Plan: Leave something in your cart today without buying it. Celebrate your self-control as if you just saved a fortune.

99

"I am embracing the fact that my hair is doing its own thing today—and it's probably winning."

No amount of product can fight Mother Nature, and today, I'll remind myself that messy hair is just a sign of a carefree spirit—or humidity's victory.

Action Plan: Rock your natural look today, whether it's wild curls, frizz, or bedhead. Call it effortless chic and own it.

100

"I am fully accepting that reheated coffee is basically just a warm hug from yesterday."

Fresh coffee is overrated when I can embrace the convenience of my trusty microwave. Today, I'll remind myself that caffeine is caffeine, no matter how old it is.

Action Plan: Reheat your coffee guilt-free. Toast to the energy boost and call it vintage brewing.

Closing Thoughts

Congratulations! You've made it through 100 affirmations, countless eye rolls, and probably a few muttered "that's so me" moments. Remember, life isn't about being perfect—it's about showing up, laughing at your chaos, and pretending you've got it all together (even when you don't).

The world is already serious enough, so don't forget to sprinkle a little sarcasm and humor into your day. Take these affirmations with you—not too seriously, of course—and use them as reminders that you're doing just fine, mismatched socks and all.

So go forth with confidence, wit, and maybe a snack in hand. You've got this—well, at least as much as anyone else does. Fake it till you make it, champ!